God Talks In Ténèk Too

(the story of Fernando Angeles)

By

Yvonne Blake

Copyright © 2014

Published by Polliwog Pages

All rights reserved.

ISBN:1496032535
ISBN-13:9781496032539

Dedicated to Ross Hodsdon -
a fervent and faithful man

CONTENTS

1	Tree to Tree	Pg 1
2	The Padre	Pg 13
3	Pancho	Pg 20
4	Going to School	Pg 24
5	Fearing God	Pg 31
6	Nando's Bible	Pg 37
7	The Jesus Movie	Pg 42
8	Bible College	Pg 47
9	Learning English	Pg 51
10	Working Together	Pg 57
	Glossary	Pg 67
	Photographs	Pg 70
	About the Author	Pg 76

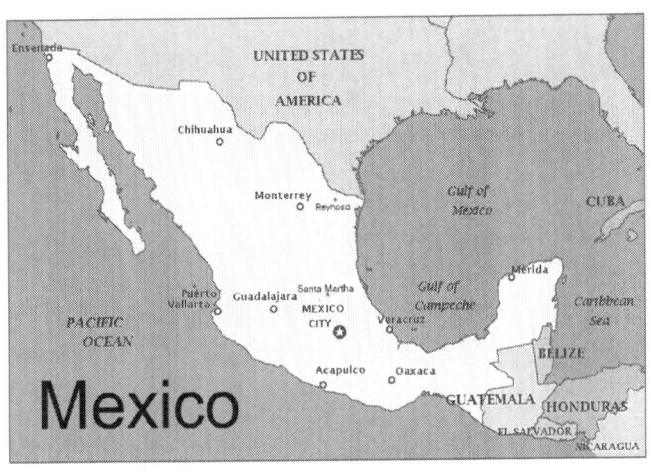

1
TREE TO TREE

"Naaaando, Naaaando!"

Fernando watched his sister approach his favorite fig tree. She squinted into the leafy branches. "Nando, I know you are up there. Mim says to get wood for the fire."

Fernando rolled his eyes. *Can't a fellow play a while?* He had spent most of the day pushing stalk after stalk into the sugarcane mill. He was tired. Fernando's toes cramped as he perched on the branch and waited for Teofila to leave.

"Naaaando!"

He hollered back, "I'll give you a glass marble if you get the wood today."

"Where'd you get a glass marble? You don't have a glass marble."

"Yes, I do. I got it from Pedro, and he got it from his cousin who lives in Santos."

"Okay, but what do I tell Mim?"

"Tell her that I say she is the best cook in Santa Martha."

Fernando turned his attention higher into the green branches. Some yellow birds flitted and chirped above him. He pulled a sling out of his pants' pocket. It was a piece of leather with a string tied on either side. He dug a pebble out of his other pocket and wrapped the leather around it.

Climbing to a higher branch, he found room to swing his arm. A plump pigeon sat nearby. He braced himself and readied his arm. A twig fell on his head, and he looked up to see a big squirrel above him. A squirrel would be tastier than a pigeon. He twirled his sling around and around and let one string loose. The stone shot through the air, but the squirrel leaped to another branch. "*Uchá!*" he grumbled.

Fernando watched the squirrel fling itself from the tree, its paws outstretched. It caught the branch of the next tree and scampered along a critter pathway. *What fun it would be to fly from tree to tree like a squirrel!*

Fernando shimmied to the end of the branch. Clutching a nearby limb, he pulled it back and then swung out over the bushes. Below him, a sheep paused in mid-chew to see him fly over his head. "WHEEEEE" He felt like a bird.

The twigs and leaves of the next tree smashed into his

face, and he frantically clutched at them. He gasped as the branch bent low under his weight, but he made it. Scrambling through the tree limbs, he launched himself to another tree and then another. *Who wants to walk on the ground, when you can fly through the air?*

Fernando paused and looked down at his uncle's bamboo house. The chickens looked like sparrows. Even the cows looked like dogs. He could see Teofila gathering wood. A flicker of guilt passed over him, but he smiled at the thought of his new skill.

Fernando scanned the area for another tree to continue his adventure. The next one was a little farther away, but he thought he could make it. Pulling back the branch as far as it would flex, he sailed through the air. As he grabbed at the leaves, one hand slipped, and he felt his shoulder POP as it took the full force of his weight. A yell of pain echoed through the village.

That evening, Fernando whimpered on his bed as he waited for Tata to come home. His grandmother hovered nearby, washing his face with water. Each time he moved, spasms of pain jolted through his shoulder. He half hoped and half feared for his father to come.

Tata shouted. "Nando, you are lazy and foolish. Now you

can't use your arm. You can't help in the fields with a crippled arm."

Poor Fernando. He felt miserable. The top of his arm bone hung loose beneath his skin. Every time he bumped it, a sharp pain shot up into his neck. Each day his shoulder got redder and more swollen.

Finally, Tata took Fernando to the village of Tanquián to find a doctor. Fernando clutched his arm to his side as Tata put him on the donkey. Usually the eight miles to Tanquián was an easy walk, but today the constant jostling was torture.

When they got to the village, the doctor squeezed Fernando's shoulder and lifted his arm. "Ow!" The doctor put his bare foot against Fernando's side. He grabbed his arm and pulled. Fernando screamed. It felt like his whole arm would fall off.

The doctor shrugged. "I can't do anything. He will be a cripple all his life."

Tata grumbled and cursed and slapped some coins in the doctor's hand. As they stepped into the street, a man standing there said, "I know someone who can help the boy. Come with me." They followed him down one street and another. "This man is an *huesero*. He fixes bones of animals. He is a good man."

The *huesero* was busy with a sheep when they arrived. They watched him massage the animal's leg and wrap it with cloths. Finally, he looked up at Tata and Fernando. "So how did the boy hurt his arm?"

Tata said. "This stupid boy thinks he can fly in the trees like the squirrels. Now he is crippled and will never be able to work again."

"Calm down, *Señor*. Sit down, and have some coffee while I look at him." He turned to Fernando. "Come, boy. Let me see your arm. So you like to climb trees, yes?"

Fernando hung his head. "When I jumped from one tree to another, I grabbed the branch and my arm popped like the leg of a grasshopper."

The *huesero* rubbed Fernando's shoulder. He rubbed his neck. It relaxed Fernando's muscles and felt good. "*Señor*, hold the boy's feet." Another man held Fernando's good arm. He whimpered in fear. The *huesero* yanked up on his arm. The pain exploded, and Fernando collapsed unconscious.

When he awoke, Fernando felt his shoulder. It was sore, but the pain was gone. Tata paid the *huesero* fifty centavos. Fernando was sorry Tata had to pay so much money. He wasn't trying to be lazy and foolish. He didn't want to be a bad boy. He'd just have to be more careful the next time he flew with the squirrels.

2
THE PADRE

"Nando, Felipe!" Tata shook their shoulders. "*Ejtsin,* Wake up, you lazy boys!" Fernando blinked at the sunbeams squeezing through the bamboo poles. "Get out of bed and catch a chicken for your mother before you go to the church school."

Fernando's eyes popped open. He didn't have to work in the fields with Tata today! A new priest had come to the village to see if they were learning their Sunday *doctina* lessons. Fernando remembered his first day. He had been only four years old.

~ ~ ~

That first time, Fernando huddled close to Felipe as they entered the big doors. He gazed at the picture of the Holy Mary and the big gold cross. The children squished together on a bench. A man in a long robe, with a cross hanging around his neck, smiled at them.

"*Hola, niños.*" (Hello, boys)

"*Hola, Padre.*" (Hello, Father)

Fernando looked from the priest to his big brother as the conversation continued for a few minutes. He wondered, "What are they saying? Why didn't the priest talk like everyone else?"

The morning was long and confusing to Fernando. The priest chanted a string of strange words from a big book. "*Dominus pascit me nihil mihi deerit in pascuis herbarum adclinavit me super aquas refectionis enutrivit me . . .*" (Psalm 23) He waved his hand from his head to his chest and then from one shoulder to the other and the children did the same.

Next, the priest asked some questions, and the children answered in unison. Fernando didn't know what they were saying. Finally, the long morning was done. Fernando shouted as he rushed through the open doors, back into the sunshine and voices that he understood.

"Felipe, why does the priest talk funny?"

"He's talking Spanish, Silly, just like the radio."

"It doesn't sound like the radio to me. Do you know what he says?"

"Most of the time . . . but not the words from the Holy Bible. They are in Latin."

"Why is the Holy Bible in Latin? Is that how God talks?"

"I don't know. That's just the way it is. The Padre knows what it says, and he tells us in Spanish because he doesn't know how to talk Ténck. I want to learn Spanish. That's how they talk in the big cities."

Fernando tried to stand as tall as his big brother. "I want to learn Spanish, too!"

Each Sunday, an adult from the village taught the children *doctina* lessons. At first, it was very confusing for little Fernando.

The teacher asked, "*¿Quien te hizo?*"

Fernando whispered to Felipe, "What did she say?"

"Who-made-you?"

The older children chanted in unison, "*Dios me hizo.*"

"Felipe, what's that mean?" Nando whispered.

"God-made-me. Now, sh-sh-sh."

As Fernando listened to the questions and answers each week, he soon learned how to respond. He was learning Spanish!

"*¿Dónde está Dios?*" (Where is God?)

"*Dios está en todas partes.*" (God is everywhere.) God being everywhere was somewhat spooky to Fernando.

"*¿Sabe Dios y ver todas las cosas?*" (Does God know and see all things?)

"*Dios sabe y ve todas las cosas, incluso nuestros pensamientos más secretos.*" (God knows and sees all things, even our most secret thoughts.)

Fernando didn't want God to know everything he did or thought, especially when he got angry with his little brother Pablo for using his sling. Maybe God only knows Spanish thoughts. He decided to only be angry in Ténel, since God doesn't talk Tének.

~ ~ ~

Fernando wouldn't be afraid of the priest this year. He stuffed a corn tortilla in his mouth and followed Felipe to the whitewashed walls of the church. No other building was as nice or as strong as their Catholic church.

A few weeks ago, the whole village had begun preparing for the new priest. They raked the roads and filled the holes with dirt. Uncle Lucio headed up a crew to build an outhouse, because it wasn't right for a holy man to use the forest like an ordinary person.

The children stood inside the big wooden doors of the church. Even their soft footsteps echoed in the large room. A shaft of sunlight made the golden crucifix glow. Fernando couldn't take his eyes from the statue of the body on the cross. He knew it was Jesus, the Son of God, who died for the wickedness of the whole world.

Fernando jumped when a man got up from his knees at the front of the church. The priest smiled at them and clutched his hands together in front of his rather round middle. Again, the priest read from the Holy Bible in Latin. He asked some *doctina* questions. This time, Fernando knew the answers and boldly answered with the other children. "Pleased with their knowledge, the priest blessed them and let them leave.

"Felipe, Padre Louis is fat, isn't he? He looks like a pregnant cow!"

Felipe's eyes twinkled. "Sh-sh, Nando, don't talk bad about the priest or Tata will give you a beating."

Fernando looked around. "Here comes Padre Louis now."

He smiled at the boys. "*Buenos dias!*" (Good day!)

Felipe and Fernando grinned. "*Buenos dias, Padre.*"

The boys crouched in the bushes and watched the priest waddle through the village, stopping occasionally to greet the grannies and pat the babies on their heads.

Fernando smiled. "Look, he's going to the outhouse. He won't fit. He's too fat."

"Sh-sh," warned Felipe, but he grinned with anticipated glee.

They were not disappointed. With hands over their mouths to suppress their laughter, they watched the round form of Padre Louis squeeze through the small door of the new outhouse.

"What are you boys doing?" said a voice behind them.

Fernando and Felipe jumped. They turned to see Teofila.

"God will make a *dhin tso'* attack you for laughing at the

priest."

Fernando wasn't afraid of a wildcat, but he was afraid of a beating.

"Don't tell Mim or Tata."

"I ought to, but I won't if you carry the water for me."

Year after year, the priest came. Fernando grew taller, learned more, and did what was expected of him. He wanted God to let him into heaven when he died. One time, Fernando thought he would die.

3
PANCHO

Fernando loved horses. He loved their strong legs and big heads. He even liked the way they smelled. Someday, he would have his own horse. Tata promised.

One day, Tsiuw, their mare, had a colt. Tata said Fernando could keep the colt if he taught it to pull a wagon and turn the sugarcane press. Fernando was so happy. He rubbed the colt's nose. "I will name you Pancho. That's a good name for you."

Pancho grew strong and beautiful, and Fernando couldn't wait until the horse was big enough to ride. Right now, he had to be satisfied with old Tsiuw as she plodded around and around, turning the sugarcane mill. Chickens ran between the mare's feet, looking for grain and bugs. Sometimes, Fernando even let his little brother, Pablo, ride on her back. Tsiuw was slow. Sometimes, she was too slow for Fernando.

Maybe he was grumpy because a buzzing mosquito pestered him all night— or maybe it was because his friends were going fishing without him, but instead of gently flicking Tsiuw with the switch, he gave her a smack on the rump. That old horse let her hind foot fly and hit him square in the belly.

Fernando lay still. He could hardly breathe. He gasped and coughed and held his belly. He leaned against the wall for a few minutes before hobbling home. His mother was mixing cornmeal for tortillas.

"Nando? What's the matter with you?"

"Tsiuw kicked me."

"That horse is getting old. We should sell her."

"No, Mim. It's my fault. I hit her too hard."

Fernando lay curled on his bed for many days. Tata was angry because Fernando couldn't work. Fernando's belly was swollen and purple. It hurt to sit up. His skin felt hot, but he shivered with cold. He didn't even want to eat.

After a week, Mim brought Fernando to the witch doctor. The hut was dark and smelled like smoldering grass. There were candles everywhere, and Mim put some coins before a statue. Fernando shivered, partly from the fever and partly in fear of what the witchdoctor might do.

The witchdoctor had a necklace of bones and a black cloth tied around his forehead. He waved a smoking stick over Fernando's belly, chanting strange words. "There is something in your stomach. The horse has kicked the bone of a chicken into you."

The witchdoctor put a bamboo tube on Fernando's belly and sucked hard. He pushed hard. It hurt! The witchdoctor sucked and sucked. He then spit a small bone into his hand and showed it to Mim and Fernando. "This is what was poisoning you." He threw it aside and sucked more, then spit on the ground. "The evil poison is gone. You will be better soon."

Then the witch doctor dipped a leafy branch in water and slapped it over Fernando's head and face and belly and legs, all the while saying strange words. "Now you are cleansed. You can go home."

Fernando's belly still hurt. It was a whole month before he felt well enough to work in the fields again. He didn't think the witchdoctor knew how to make him better.

There never seemed to be enough money. Fernando's

family grew corn for tortillas and raised chickens, but if they wanted salt or rice, they must buy it at the market. Tata never seemed to have enough money for his liquor. Mim complained that he took her blankets and pans to pay for his whiskey.

Mim treasured her bee hives. The bees gathered nectar from the forest flowers and brought it back to the hive to make honey. She even used the bees' larvae to make *wat'ap*, a hot porridge. Fernando got tired of eating *wat'ap* every morning, but it was food.

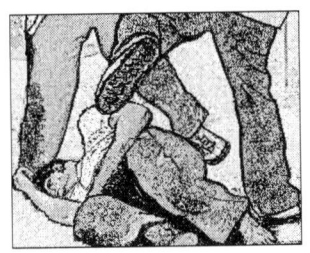

4
GOING TO SCHOOL

Tata didn't sell Pancho. Fernando didn't know how he got the money to buy shoes, but he bought some. Tata and Fernando walked for two days through the mountains to San Vicente. Fernando wasn't sure he wanted to go to school. He would have to wear a white shirt and shoes every day. He hated his shoes. His feet felt trapped, like a pig with its head stuck in a pail. He took them off, tied the strings together, and wore them over his shoulder. He didn't have to wear them yet.

When they got to San Vicente, Tata led Fernando past rows of painted houses until they came to a blue one on the edge of town. It had a red tiled roof and glass windows. This is where Fernando would live. He would earn his keep by gathering wood or carrying water. Tata left without looking back. Fernando felt all alone.

School began the next day. His heart thumped as he followed the other children through the streets. There were many cars and trucks. Loud music played from radios. Fernando tried to read the signs on the stores. Many children in white shirts and shoes entered a building. Fernando went with them, but he felt alone.

The classroom was even bigger than his bamboo house back in the mountains. Rows of desks faced a bigger desk at the front. Fernando knew some of the Spanish words on the blackboard. He sat near the wall and watched the other students arrive.

A group of boys strode into the room and claimed the desks in the back corner. The tallest boy, José, seemed to be their leader. The others laughed at whatever he said. Fernando noticed José looking at him. José whispered something, and all the other boys laughed. The teacher came in, and the students settled into their seats.

The day was confusing. Fernando didn't understand much. He knew it was Spanish, but the teacher talked fast, and the words sounded different. The city kids laughed at Fernando when he said the wrong word. The teacher laughed, too, and made him feel stupid. He was glad when it was finally time to go home – well, back to the blue house. He couldn't wait to take off his shoes. He hung them over his shoulder and headed toward the door.

"Hey, Barefoot Boy, are you lost?"

It was José. The other boys laughed. Fernando ducked his head. He hoped José would leave him alone.

"Hey, look at me! This school for big boys."

Fernando kept his eyes down.

"Why don't you go home to your mama – where nobody cares if you are barefoot or NOT." With the last word, José stomped on Fernando's toe with his heavy boot.

Fernando clenched his jaw to hold back a cry. He swung his fist, but José caught his arm.

"Ahhh . . . did I make the baby mad? Are you going to cry?"

Fernando swung again, but José grabbed him around the waist and carried him upside down out of the building. Fernando squirmed and hollered for help, but the other boys only laughed. José dropped him onto the road and gave him a kick in the pants.

"That's where you belong, *Tonto!*"

Fernando stood up. He was crying, not because he was hurt, but because he was angry. He put his head down and charged like a bull at José, knocking him to the ground. He punched José over and over. "I am not *tonto*! I am not *tonto*!"

The two boys rolled and kicked in the dirt. José stood up and grabbed Fernando's new white shirt. Fernando felt it rip. José punched him in the stomach. Fernando fell backwards, but stood up again. José pushed and pushed until Fernando was up against the wall. The other boys circled around, their eyes glimmering with anticipation of seeing a Tének, a *sin razón* (a person without reasoning) get a beating.

Fernando's back bumped against the concrete wall. His eyes held José's gaze while his hand groped for a weapon. He felt a pole. He glanced at it – a mop! As José stepped closer, Fernando pulled the mop from behind his back. He swung it to his left! He swung it to the right! He hit their heads and their backs and their bellies. He didn't care what he hit. Soon he was just swinging at the air. They had all left.

Fernando leaned against the wall and laid his head on his knees. Maybe they'd leave him alone now. Maybe now he could show them that he wasn't *tonto*.

Fernando hated being in San Vicente. Once, on his way to school, a rotten mango hit him in the head. Its pulp got in his hair. The juice ran down his neck and on his white shirt. The children laughed at him at school. The teacher scolded him. "Fernando Angeles, that may be how you dress in your village, but not here. I want you to wear shoes and clean clothes when you come to school."

Fernando heard snickers from José and his friends. He slumped in his chair, crossed his arms. *I don't care what they think of me* ... but he did care.

Fernando walked home to his family every weekend. On Sundays, when it was time to go back to school, he wished he could stay home and work in Tata's field instead of going back to school in San Vicente.

Every morning in school, they started with the Lord's Prayer. "*Padre nuestro, que estas en los cielos* ..." (Our Father, which art in heaven ...) He mumbled along until he noticed Lucas had a new haircut. His bare neck showed above his collar.

Fernando picked up a piece of sand from the floor and flicked it with his fingers. "*Uchál!*" He missed! He tried again. This one hit Lucas's neck.

Lucas spun around. "Stop that!"

Fernando innocently quoted the next line in the prayer.

"*Perdona nuestras ofensas...*" (Forgive us our trespasses . . .) He didn't want to think about his trespasses. As soon as Lucas turned forward again, Fernando flicked another piece of sand.

Lucas raised his hand. Fernando kicked his chair and whispered, "If you tell, I'll beat you up." Lucas put his hand down, and Fernando smiled. Maybe if he acted tough, the big boys wouldn't pick on him. Maybe things would be better, but they weren't.

José was a constant pest. Every day he called Fernando names and made the other boys laugh. Fernando didn't care. He noticed that José didn't get good grades. Fernando decided he could be better than José by getting the best scores in the class. He would show them that he was not *tonto*.

~ ~ ~

Fernando was glad when he was old enough to go to high school. The school was in Tanquián. He would be able to go home each day to be with his family. Fernando enjoyed learning about other places and people. He studied hard and made good grades.

The spring of his last year was very rainy. One day, a big mudslide blocked the road back to Santa Martha. A man came to the school and announced, "Those of you who live down the mountain should not walk home tonight. It is too dangerous. You can sleep in the Catholic church."

The wooden pews were not very comfortable, and Fernando couldn't sleep. He could hear two priests talking nearby. Fernando was shocked and disgusted with the things he heard. *Someone who teaches about God should not be doing such wicked things.* Fernando couldn't wait for morning to come, so he could go home.

5
FEARING GOD

"Nando!" Uncle Lucio staggered up to him with a bottle in his hand. "You have finished high school. You can read Spanish, yes?" He shoved a package in Fernando's face. "I have a present for you . . . a book."

Fernando looked at the coverless collection of pages. "What kind of book is it?"

"It is a good book – a book for a priest."

"Have you read it?"

"No, I can't read, but you can. You take it. It is a good book."

Fernando tucked it in his shirt to look at later. His uncle slapped his shoulder and Fernando laughed. It was a night to celebrate.

The next morning, Fernando looked at the tattered book. It was a Holy Bible, but it was Spanish – not Latin. "*El nacimiento de Jesucristo fue de esta manera...*" (Matthew 1) Fernando read on and on. He read of Jesus healing the sick and walking on the water. He had heard some of these stories in his Sunday *doctina* classes, but he was hungry to learn more ... hungry with an empty heart.

"Angelo," Fernando said to his friend, "Listen to this, **'Many will say to me in that day, Lord, Lord, have we not prophesied in your name? and in your name have cast out devils? and in your name done many wonderful works? and then will I profess unto them, I never knew you; depart from me, you workers of iniquity.'** (Matthew 7:22,23) Will God say, '*Apartaos de mí*' to good people? Are doing good things not enough?"

"Nando, you are talking like a Protestant. You will be cursed."

"Angelo, doesn't your heart feel dirty with sin? I'm afraid of God. I want to know how He will let me into heaven."

"Nando, leave it alone. It will only bring you trouble."

However, the words in the book wouldn't leave Fernando alone. He fished and hunted and worked in the fields ... but the words echoed in his mind. *"Apartaos de mí, apartaos de mí."* Fernando couldn't think of anything else. His family and friends shook their heads and hoped he would forget this crazy thinking.

One afternoon, lightning flashed and thunder rumbled. Fernando shivered at the dark clouds. He didn't want to die. He didn't want to hear God to say, "Depart from me." The rain poured on the dusty ground. Streams of water ran down the roads, and drips plopped through the thatched roof. The sky darkened. Everyone sat around and listened to the storm.

Ramirez, their neighbor, burst into their house. "Señora, I am sorry to tell you, but your husband is dead!"

Mim covered her face. "Nooooo! Where is he?"

"I saw him in the creek by Gonzales' shack. I'm sorry, Señora."

Gonzales sold liquor in a shanty on the edge of his fields. It was illegal, but he had plenty of customers. Fernando's father and others often bought his bottles of whisky.

Fernando and Felipe knew they must get Tata's body, but they were afraid. Uncle Juan and their cousin, Chano, went with them. They walked along the washed-out creek bed. The rain had stopped, but the night was dark. Occasionally, lightning flashed. Fernando shivered.

Felipe saw their father first. He was lying in the sandy creek bed, amid mud and sticks and leaves. Chano wailed, "Oh, Uncle! Why did you die?" He cleared the debris from Tata's face. Fernando wanted to run.

Uncle Juan and Felipe pulled Tata out of the mud. Fernando stood to the side and watched. They rolled Tata over onto his back. He groaned!

Felipe's eyes widened. "Is he a ghost?"

Uncle Juan said, "He's still alive! We need to get him warm." He grabbed Tata under his shoulders. "Come, help me carry him to Gonzales' shack." Fernando grabbed a leg. It was heavy and wet.

They dragged Tata inside and dropped him on the floor. The stench of liquor and filth filled the cabin. Uncle Juan began building a fire in the stove. "You boys take off his wet clothes. There must be something in that pile that will fit him." A mound of clothes lay in the corner. Most people traded whatever they could for liquor.

Fernando dug through the clothes. There were plenty of shoes and blankets. There were even children's clothes. Finally, he found a pair of pants. They were huge – big enough for a giant. He also found a sweater — a woman's sweater, but it would be warm.

As they pulled the sweater over his father's shoulders, Fernando saw the scar on Tata's back from another drunken episode. That time, he had passed out against the side of a truck. The sun was so hot that the metal had burned his back . . . this time, he almost drowned.

Tata looked funny in the big pants and tight sweater, but his skin was getting warmer. Uncle Juan stood up. "We will leave him here to sleep. He'll be fine."

Mim was waiting for them. Her eyes were red. Fernando said, "Mim, he's not dead. He was drunk and fell in the creek. He's still alive. We left him to sleep at Gonzales' shack. I'll go get him tomorrow if he doesn't come back himself."

The next morning, Fernando woke to the sound of voices. The neighbors, thinking Tata was dead, had come with food and candles for the burial. As Fernando retold the activities of the night, the door banged open.

Tata stood in the doorway. His bloodshot eyes stared at the crowd. Mud and leaves still clung to his hair and neck. He held up the pants with one hand. The striped sweater stretched across his chest and the sleeves only came to his elbows. "What's going on here?"

One woman said, "Ramirez said you were dead – that you drowned in the creek!"

"I'm not dead! Do you want me to be dead? Well, I'm sorry to disappoint you!" He waved his arm around. "Get out of my house. Get out!"

As the last person slunk away, Tata looked at Fernando and Mim before storming off to find another bottle of liquor.

6
NANDO'S BIBLE

One day, Fernando's friend, Roman, the son of the witch doctor, came to visit. "Nando, I have something for you. I am afraid to have this Protestant book." He glanced around before handing Fernando a small blue book with gold writing on the cover and an emblem of a flame. "Take it. If my father knew that I even touched it, he would beat me and put a curse on me."

It was a Spanish New Testament. Fernando carried his little blue Bible everywhere. He read by lamplight and by morning light. He read the whole New Testament in ten months.

It was difficult for Fernando to think with all the noise of the village – the chickens, donkeys, and children. He knew just the place to be alone. It had been a long time since he climbed the tall, leafy fig tree. From his perch, he could see down the mountain onto the rooftops of his village. He pulled the book out of his shirt.

It was very much like his tattered priests' Bible, but as he read the words, it seemed that God was talking right to him. **"I am the way, the truth and the life. No man cometh unto the Father, but by me."** (John 14:6)

He read on and on. It was different from the *doctina* classes, different from anything he heard at school. The book told him he was a sinner. He knew that. He felt the heaviness of all the times he lied and cheated and made his mother cry and his father angry. This book did not tell him to chant prayers or go to the priest. His Bible said there was nothing he could do to get to heaven by himself. Only Jesus could save him.

Fernando closed his eyes. "Jesus, I know You are the Son of God. I have read Your book. I want You to take away my sins. I want You to let me into heaven. I can't be good enough. I believe You can save me."

Fernando felt satisfied. He felt free. He felt like flying from tree to tree as he did when he was a boy. He must tell everyone what this book says. He wondered, *What will Tata and Mim say?*

At first, Fernando didn't tell anyone about praying in the tree. He didn't know what to say, but he knew something good had happened. He wasn't afraid of dying anymore. He felt clean and happy.

The next week, the priest came to Santa Martha and invited all the teenagers to some meetings. He wanted them to remember the rules of the church before they became adults. Many of the young people went, not because they cared about being good, but it was a time to get away from work and to be with their friends.

Fernando didn't feel like going. He fixed the thatched roof for his mother and cleared some weeds with his machete. His friends said, "Nando, you ought to come. Amelia is there, and she is looking very pretty!"

Fernando blushed. "Maybe tomorrow."

Fernando went on Friday, the last day. The priest reviewed all the *doctina* teachings about baptism and holy communion. Fernando knew these things in his head, but now he knew they wouldn't take him to Heaven.

The priest said, "Because you came to these meetings, now you are sanctified. If you should die right now, your sins are forgiven and you will be in purgatory for only a little while." Fernando looked up in shock. *Attending classes does not forgive sins!*

The priest left the room for a minute to get a treat. The teens began acting foolishly and teasing each other. Ricardo told a dirty joke, and everyone laughed. Fernando thought, *I must tell them what the Bible says, but what if they laugh at me?* He couldn't be quiet anymore. He stood up. "I want to tell you something."

His friends looked at him – Angelo and Roman and Amelia – thinking he would tell another joke. Fernando took a deep breath. "This is not right. The priest can't forgive your sins just because you came to these meetings. Only God can forgive your sins."

Angelo whispered, "Nando, sit down."

Some looked around nervously. This was dangerous to be speaking against the church and the priest. Others listened carefully. They hungered for the truth.

Fernando continued. "We learned the Ten Commandments in *doctina* classes together. **'Thou shalt have no other gods before me.'** We shouldn't pray to Mary. **'Thou shalt not lie.'** I know you lie. I've lied many times.

'Thou shalt not commit adultery.' 'Honor thy father and thy mother.' We're all sinners. I read it in my Bible. I asked Jesus to forgive my sins. You need to ask Him to forgive you. That's the only way to go to heaven."

It was quiet. Not knowing what to do, Fernando walked out the door. The young people were not laughing and joking anymore. He heard them tell the priest what he had said. The priest shouted, "Don't listen to Fernando. He's not a priest! What does he know? He can't understand God's Word."

7
THE JESUS MOVIE

Fernando wasn't afraid of dying anymore. He knew God had forgiven his sins. He knew no one could get to heaven by keeping all the rules of the church – not even the priests. He saw in his Bible, **"For by grace, are ye saved through faith, and that not of yourselves. It is the gift of God, not of works lest any man should boast."** (Ephesians 2:8,9)

Fernando didn't want to attend the Catholic church anymore. How could he listen to the priests teach about being good when they got drunk and took women like other men? Fernando knew there must be others that believed like him.

At first, Fernando was afraid to step into a Protestant church. Wasn't he taught from a boy that he would be cursed – that he would get sick or bitten by a snake? But his desire to find the truth was stronger than his fears.

Many churches he visited talked about Jesus and heaven, but they wanted him to be good. They said he must be baptized before he could go to heaven. They said he should be filled with the Holy Spirit and talk in God's language. He knew he didn't have to earn God's forgiveness – only to believe it.

At the mission church in Tanquián, Fernando felt welcomed. The people smiled. Someone gave him a songbook. The pastor asked the congregation to open to I Kings. Some people had Bibles. Fernando couldn't find I Kings in his blue Bible.

Pastor Benito spoke of Elijah and the priests of Baal. The forty priests shouted and prayed and even cut themselves, but their god never answered. Elijah asked for twelve barrels of water to be poured over his altar. He quietly prayed to the Lord God. A bolt of fire streaked from heaven. It burned the sacrifice, the wood, the stones, and even the water. There was no doubt which God was real. Pastor Benito quoted Joshua, **"Choose you this day whom ye will serve . . . as for me and my house, we will serve the Lord."** Fernando said to himself, "I choose to serve the Lord."

Afterward, Fernando told Pastor Benito how he had read the whole New Testament. He told about talking to God in the fig tree and looking for a church which taught that the only way to heaven was to believe in God's forgiveness of sin. Fernando knew he had found the right place.

Pastor Benito gave him a whole Bible so he could read the stories in the Old Testament of Moses and David and Elijah, too. Every week Fernando went to the mission church to hear more about this new life.

Each week, he told his family and friends what he learned. His mother and grandmother listened but didn't want to change. His father didn't want to listen at all. Some of his friends were afraid. "Nando, don't talk that way. It is dangerous." But others listened.

One Sunday, Fernando saw a movie about Jesus. *If my village could see this movie, maybe they would listen.* Pastor Benito promised to bring a projector and generator if Fernando could find a screen. Fernando hurried home. What could he use as a screen? All the walls were of bamboo. A white cloth might work if he could find one.

Night had fallen as he walked into his village, and the whitewashed walls of the Catholic church gleamed in the moonlight. *Yes! It was perfect!* He would tell everyone about the Jesus movie and ask Pastor Benito to come. Word spread quickly. "Fernando is showing a movie picture on Friday night."

On Friday, Fernando set up some benches behind the Catholic church, facing the big blank wall. Pastor Benito set up the projector. Everything was ready. As the sun sank lower, people began gathering. People came from other villages. Hundreds came to see the movie. They watched Jesus blessing the children, stilling the storm, and healing the sick. They moaned when Jesus was beaten and nailed to the tree. They shouted when he rose from the grave. Even those that didn't understand Spanish understood the pictures.

Everything went well, but there was a problem. Fernando had forgotten that it was the Friday before Easter. The priest had come to the village for the Good Friday Mass. Everybody wanted to see the movie instead of going to mass. The priest was not happy.

The next day, Fernando felt the tension in the village. To talk about his beliefs was not too bad, but to take the villagers away from the Good Friday Mass was unforgiveable. All the men of the village gathered in the council building.

"Fernando, you have disrupted our village with your Protestant beliefs. We have tolerated it until now. We hoped you would follow the ways of your father and uncles, but this has been too much."

Fernando didn't say anything. He looked at the ground, shuffled his feet in the dirt, and waited for his verdict.

Diego Santiago spoke up. "I have noticed that those who listen to Fernando have changed. They have stopped getting drunk and beating their wives. They work hard and help others. That is a good thing."

Fernando looked up at Diego with gratitude.

Uncle Juan said, "Fernando, can you assure us that you will not preach of your beliefs in a public gathering again?"

Fernando shook his head. "I can't say that. I want to tell everyone about the Gospel of Jesus Christ. I would like to start my own church."

Some of the men guffawed at the last statement. "You may go. We will tell you what we have decided."

Fernando waited days and weeks and months. He told Pastor Benito of the council. The people in the mission church prayed and waited. Nothing happened. Because the council couldn't find enough bad in Fernando's teachings, they didn't stop him from preaching.

8
BIBLE SCHOOL

Fernando wasn't sure what to do after he graduated. His father wanted him to get a good job in the city. The government sent a letter, asking him to be a teacher. He would earn a lot of money, but he wasn't sure it was God's will for him.

Fernando wanted to learn more about the Bible. Pastor Benito told him about a Bible college in Chapulhuacán. It was a long ways from Santa Martha and Tanquián, but the idea was exciting.

Tata crossed his arms. "How will you pay for this? I can't give you any money."

"I'll find a job and pay for it myself. I want to go, Tata. This is important to me."

Fernando learned that the students worked at the college to pay for their studies. He was overjoyed to be accepted. He thought it would be like heaven. Wasn't it full of people who loved God?

However, Fernando was disappointed to see that some students weren't excited about the Bible. They acted rebellious and disobeyed school rules. He was discouraged and wasn't sure he wanted to finish his studies. He decided to talk to the director.

"Fernando, do you read your Bible?"

"Yes, we read it every day in our classes."

"Do you pray?"

"Of course! We pray at chapel and at meals and in class. We pray all the time."

The director shook his head. "Fernando, you need a personal relationship with God. You need to read your Bible by yourself and pray. Just as the Holy Spirit brought you to salvation, He will teach you and help you to grow."

As Fernando spent time reading the Bible alone, the joy returned. The classes became more interesting, and his zeal to share the Gospel returned.

Each weekend, Fernando went home to Santa Martha. He read the Spanish Bible to anyone that would listen and explained it in Tének. He wished they could read the Bible themselves. *How am I any different than the priests reading in Latin and explaining it in their own words? The Tének people need to read God's Word for themselves.*

One day, Fernando sat on the ground next to Doroteo. The young man's body had been very weak from the time they were children together. He never worked in the fields or hunted with the other boys.

"Doroteo, how are you doing today?"

"I get so tired. My chest hurts when I walk too much. I listened to you talk about Jesus. Nando, will you tell me more?"

Fernando smiled. *Thank you, Lord.* He quoted John 3:16 in Tének, slowly and carefully, so that Doroteo could hear each word.

"Kom a Dios in wat'k'adh k'anidha' an k'wajchidh tsabál, kej in bína' in junkats tsakámil abal jiták'itsk'ij ki in bela' yabáts ka k'ibej po ki in ko'oy an ets'ey ejataláb""

Fernando told how Jesus had come to seek and to save

those who are lost. He told how Jesus could heal the sick and forgive sins. No one could be good enough to be saved. Each one must believe in God's gift of forgiveness and eternal life. Doroteo was the first to believe the words of the Gospel.

Every week, a truck drove through the villages to take people to Tanquián. Most people chose to walk rather than pay the fifty centavos. Those who rode crowded into the back of the truck.

Doreteo was not strong enough to walk over the mountains. One Saturday, he wanted to go to Tanquián, but the truck was ready to leave. Doreteo ran up the hill and scrambled into the back just in time. He lay there, gasping for breath and clutching his chest. Then he was still. The passengers hollered at the driver to stop. Everyone was quiet. Doreteo had died.

When Fernando heard the news, he was very sad . . . yet he could tell the others that Doreteo was not in purgatory. He was not sick anymore but in heaven with God. Many people listened to Fernando and believed in Christ.

9
LEARNING ENGLISH

When Fernando finished Bible college, he was now 26 years old, but he still didn't feel ready to start a church. A man named Mel Moody heard about Fernando and invited him to come to Dublin Christian Academy in New Hampshire.

Fernando nervously strapped the seatbelt over his lap. He had rarely ridden in a car, and now he would be flying. When the flight attendant came by, he looked through the cards that Mel Moody sent him. He handed her the one with *"avion"* in the corner. It had words in English, but he didn't know what they said. PLEASE GIVE ME A COKE, AND DON'T FORGET THE PEANUTS. He wondered why she laughed.

When they landed, Fernando's legs felt like pudding. The air was very cold. He hunkered his head into his collar. He couldn't understand English. He was grateful that Kevin

Moody met him at the airport. At the school, the staff and students were friendly, but he felt alone and far from home.

Bill, the janitor, assigned Fernando the job of driving the tractor and taught him some English words - "leaves," "rake," and "shed." Each day Fernando learned more, but sometimes they just weren't enough.

Fernando didn't mind picking up trash and mowing the lawns, but the November winds were freezing. He bundled in sweaters and gloves and scarves and a hat until only his eyes showed, and he wished he could cover them, too. Suddenly, the tractor stopped. It was out of gas. He tromped from building to building to find Bill.

"Hey, Fernando! Are you finished?"

"No . . . problem."

"A problem? What's wrong?"

"Gasoline"

"You ran out of gas?"

Fernando smiled. With a red container of gas, Fernando headed out into the wind again. He took off his gloves to open the frozen cap. Finally, it came off. Fernando started to pour the gas when he realized it was the wrong place. It was the radiator! He replaced the cover and found the gas tank. *Maybe a little bit won't matter.*

By the time he finished filling the gas tank, he thought his fingers would fall off. He turned the key. Smoke billowed from the tractor. Fernando shut it off. He tried again. Again, smoke poured from the engine. Fernando sighed. He tromped across campus . . . again . . . to find Bill.

"How's it going, Fernando?"

"Problem"

"What kind of problem?"

Fernando knew what was wrong, but he didn't know how to say it. All he could say was, "problem" and motion for Bill to follow. He wished he knew more words.

Winter arrived. Fernando had never seen snow. He had fun making it into snowballs, but it was so cold. One night, when he returned from a meeting, Fernando ran through the bitter air toward his dormitory. He slipped on the snow-covered sidewalk and fell backwards, hitting his head. By the time he opened his eyes again, a layer of snow covered him. He had a headache for a long time and learned not to run in the snow again.

As the weeks went by, Fernando learned more and more English and more about the Bible. It was good to be with others who loved the Lord. They gave him an English Bible, but it was hard for him to understand. Now he had three Bibles, but none of them were in Ténex. He liked to study, and the teachers were patient and helpful. He was eager to go home and share the things he had learned.

One day, Kevin Moody asked, "Fernando, have you heard of the Bible camp in Monterrey, Mexico?"

Fernando shook his head.

"I think you'd like it. Since you know Spanish already, you'd be a great help."

Before long, he was flying back to Mexico. Airplanes still frightened him, but he was anxious to go home. He missed the quiet forests and the simple ways of life.

"Nando!"

"Hey, Pablo, you are taller than I am now!"

It was good to be home. His house seemed much smaller than he remembered. His grandmother seemed much thinner and older. She gave him a toothless grin and patted the bench for him to sit down. "You were a good boy, yes? Did you learn many things?"

"Yes, I can read books in English now."

"You are a smart boy."

Pablo showed him the new *borrego* (lamb). Mim brought him some water, and his sisters smiled as they fried tortillas. Fernando was happy to be home. Tata entered the kitchen and looked hard at Fernando. "Did you get a job and lots of money in America?"

Fernando hung his head. "No, Tata. I had a job, but it only paid for the school. I didn't bring much back."

His father's eyes darkened. "Are you going to stay home now and work in the fields? Maybe you will find a good wife and have a family!"

Fernando blushed. "I will help you while I'm home, but I plan to work at a Baptist camp this summer. Maybe Pablo can come with me?"

"What is this camp?"

"They teach the young people about God."

"You'll live at this camp?"

"The young people stay for a week. I will stay for a few

months."

Tata crossed his arms. "Pablo needs to help me in the fields."

Fernando nodded his head. He knew it was a busy time at home. He knew his father feared Pablo would also go away.

10
WORKING TOGETHER

At the camp in Monterrey, counselors came from all over the United States and Mexico. One girl had long black hair and dark eyes and a very pretty smile. Her name was Christy. By the end of the summer, Fernando asked Christy if he could write to her.

For five years, he wrote to her. Fernando told her how he wanted to teach the people in his village about God. He told her that Pastor Benito had said, "You ought to be in a big Spanish church, Fernando. Your little village doesn't have enough money to pay you." He told how he had begun preaching at a church in Tamazunchale.

Fernando asked Christy to pray for him. He was still thinking of those in Santa Martha that still did not have salvation. He saw missionaries come from the United States and learn Spanish to be able to preach in Mexico. He told her, "I already know the Ténex language. Why should someone else learn Ténex to be a missionary to my people? I need to go home and start a church in Santa Martha myself."

Fernando was glad that Christy was interested in the native people of Mexico. He wondered if she was the girl God wanted him to marry. He wanted a wife that loved God and would love his people, too.

Each summer at camp, Fernando saw Christy, but he was too shy to talk to her about love. He prayed for wisdom. Finally, Fernando wrote Christy and asked her to marry him. She replied that he should talk to her parents first. Christy lived in Hawaii. That was half way around the world.

This was very important to Fernando. It was right, and it was good, but how could he afford to fly all the way to Hawaii? He would have to sell his cows. As Fernando packed his clothes, he prayed, "Lord, this is all in Your hands. If You want me to marry Christy, let her parents like me. Lord, show me Your will for my life."

Hawaii was nice, but not as beautiful as Christy. Her parents welcomed him into their home and had many things to ask him. They questioned him for four hours. They asked about his childhood and schooling and how he might deal with certain situations. He hoped they liked his answers, but it was all in God's hands.

Fernando and Christy were very happy when her parents gave their approval. They were married on June 26, 2004. Christy was anxious to see his village. Finally, he took her to Santa Martha to meet his family. He told Christy that his people were very quiet and shy, not as open and happy as she was. She might have to hold back her enthusiasm if she wanted them to like her. She tried, but she couldn't. It wasn't in her nature to be quiet. He was surprised that everyone liked her bubbly personality.

It was the custom of his people that if you said *"Nenek"* (Hello) to a person in the morning, you didn't greet them again later in the day. Christy didn't follow their custom. She said, *"Nenek"* to them as many times as she saw them that day. The people didn't mind. They said *"Nenek"* back to her with a smile. Fernando was glad they liked Christy.

Christy had other problems with the language, too. One of the first words she learned to say was *tsiuw*. She thought it meant "cute" because whenever Fernando saw any animal, he would say, *"tsiuw bichum* (horse), *tsiuw olom* (pig), etc." Christy didn't know that it meant "stinky." She saw a little puppy and said, *"Tsiuw pikó"* which meant "stinky dog." The villagers laughed at her learning to talk Ténck.

The word *kalám* means "see you on the morrow" and *k'alam* means "pumpkin." One day, Christy told someone, "See you on the pumpkin." Fernando's family loved Christy and patiently taught her to speak their language.

The Mexican government began developing a written language for the Tének, and it was taught in the schools. Children read stories and textbooks in Tének, but they still didn't have a Bible in their language.

Together, Fernando and Christy planned how they would start translating God's Word into Tének. It was hard work. Sometimes there wasn't a word in Tének for the one in the Bible. They wanted it to be true, not just what they thought it meant. Fernando knew that he needed to learn Greek and maybe Hebrew for the Old Testament.

Pastor Benito said, "There are translation organizations in the United States. Ask the Lord to show you the right one."

Fernando and Christy searched and prayed. Bibles International looked very good. They thought this organization might have a book that would help them. They were so happy to learn that Bibles International would teach them how to translate. The mission sent consultants to train them and to check their work. Bibles International would also print the Bibles when they were done translating. Fernando and Christy thanked God for answering their prayers.

Fernando traveled many miles over rough roads and through the mountains to tell the Ténex people about Jesus. It was always dangerous to travel in those remote places. There were many wicked men who had guns. They wore masks over their faces so that no one would know who they were. Sometimes the militia men stopped cars or trucks to look for drugs or guns. Sometimes rebels and drug dealers killed people, but Fernando knew that God was taking care of him.

Fernando wanted to make a good home for Christy. He didn't want her to live in a bamboo house with a grass roof and dirt floors. He made a strong house of cement with tile floors and a strong roof. He made a place for a committee to work together on translating the Bible into Ténex. He put a long fence all around his land.

One day, a neighbor told him, "Each night, a van with dark windows sits at your gate. It is not good."

Fernando said, "God will take care of us."

He and Christy prayed to God for protection. They prayed for the men who were watching their house at night. After a few nights, the van stopped coming. Nothing bad happened. God protected them.

Fernando and Christy got up early each morning to pray for the people of Santa Martha. Many drank liquor and beat their wives and children. Some thought the witch doctor could help their sicknesses. All were afraid of the militia and drug gangs. Evil was all around them, but God was working in the hearts of the Ténekpeople.

It was the time of *Dia de los Muertos,* or Days of the Dead. For this religious celebration, people visited the cemetery where their loved ones were buried. They decorated gravesites with marigold flowers and candles. They brought toys for dead children and bottles of liquor to adults. They sat on blankets next to gravesites and ate the favorite food of their loved ones. It made Fernando and Christy sad to see so many who did not know the God of life.

One Sunday, as Fernando and Christy walked to their church building, Christy was delighted to see Ibet, a girl who had been to Bible Club, walking with her mother.

"*Nenek,* Ibet! Would you like to come to Sunday School sometime?"

"We are going to Tanquian to buy things for the *Dia de los Muertos*," said the mother. "but may I come to the church sometime?"

Christy and Fernando were very happy and told the times of the meetings. Maria and Ibet went on their way, only to return about ten minutes later. They stayed for the whole meeting. God must have been working in Maria's heart, for she did not go to Tanquian that day.

~ ~ ~

One time, Fernando and Christy took a trip to the United States to attend a Bible conference and translation workshop. God enabled them to accomplish much on their Bible translation, and they were anxious to get back home and continue their work.

While they were in the village of Reynosa, near the border of Mexico and the United States, they took the time to register their truck. It should have taken only one or two hours, but they had to wait all day at the office. At the end, the government office didn't return Fernando's Mexican ID – the people at the office had lost it. After another hour, they finally found the ID, but by then, it was getting late. It wasn't safe to travel after dark.

Fernando and Christy knew that God is always in control. They prayed. Fernando had a niece named Sara, who lived in Reynosa. They decided to ask if they could spend the night with her. They found Sara in her tattoo shop, where she was negotiating with a young man. While Fernando waited, he prayed for the young man. He didn't know until later that the man was a member of a drug gang.

The next morning, Fernando and Christy drove through the rugged mountains. Rounding a corner, Fernando slammed on the brakes. A van with dark windows was blocking the road. Christy prayed, "Oh Lord, help us!" Men with guns walked toward them. Christy grabbed Fernando's hand. "Lord, protect us!"

One man with a mask over his face leaned over and looked in the window of their truck. He looked at Fernando and Christy. He didn't make them get out. He didn't even ask them for their money. He said, "*Buenos Dias!*" and motioned them to go on.

Fernando laughed, and Christy cheered. "Thank you, Lord." God had protected them. They didn't know why; they didn't know how, but God showed His power and protected them from harm.

Another Sunday, while Christy was teaching some

children that came to Sunday school, a little girl named Lili – only two years old – picked up a Spanish Gospel tract and stared at its pictures. Christy said, "Do you want to hear the story about the picture?"

Christy told the story of Jesus coming to earth because He loved us so much. Christy spoke loudly enough for all the children to hear her. She told them that even though we are all sinners and deserve God's punishment, Jesus took our punishment for us. She didn't know someone else was listening.

A young boy named Kevin was waiting for his grandfather to come out of a nearby store. He sat on the other side of the fence and heard everything Christy said. Kevin wanted so much know about the pictures that he finally called out, "Let me see! I want to see!"

"Who is that?" said Christy. "Come around the fence to our Sunday School."

"I have to wait for my grandfather. He'll be angry if I went to your church class."

"Can you come next week?"

"I will be going back to my home next week."

Christy slipped a Gospel tract through the fence for him. She prayed that Kevin would find someone to read it to him. She prayed that he would learn of God's salvation.

As Fernando translated sections of God's Word, he printed some of it for Bible studies. The young people, who had learned to read in school, were excited. They invited many of their friends to come to the Bible classes and camps.

Rosa, one girl who had accepted God's gift of salvation, loved reading it in her own language. With each new verse she said, "Oh, so that's what it means!"

As Fernando watched Rosa bending over the verses, he thought, "God is speaking in Téncek." He looked forward to the day when the whole Bible would be in the language of his people.

GLOSSARY
(in order of appearance)

Ténhek Words

Mim – Mom

Tata – Dad

Uchál! – Oh no! (negative interjection)

Ejtsin! – Wake up!

dhin tso' – wild cat

wat'ap – porridge made with bee larva

"Kom a Dios in wat'k'adh k'anidha' an k'wajchidh tsabál, kej in bína' in junkats tsakámil abal jiták'itsk'ij ki in bela' yabáts ka k'ibej po ki in ko'oy an ets'ey ejataláb" – (John 3:16) "For God so loved the world, that He gave His only begotten Son, that whosoever believeth in Him should not perish but have everlasting life."

Nenek – Hello

tsiuw – stinky

bichum – horse

olom – pig

pikó – dog

kalám – on the next day

k'alam – pumpkin

Spanish Words

huesero – bone doctor (especially for animals)

Señor – Mister

doctina – religious/doctrinal

Padre – Catholic priest/Father

Hola - Hello

niños – boys

"**¿Quien te hizo?**" – "Who made you?"

"**Dios me hizo.**" – "God made me."

"**¿Dónde está Dios?**" – "Where is God?"

"**Dios esta en todas partes.**" – "God is everywhere."

"**¿Sabe Dios y ver todas las cosas?**" – "Does God know everything?"

"**Dios sabe y ve todas las cosas, incluso nuestros

pensamientos más secretos." –

"God knows everything, even your secret thoughts."

"Buenos dias!" – "Have a good day!"

Tonto! – Stupid!

Sin razón – a person without reasoning

"Padre nuestro, que estás en los cielos . . . " – "Our Father, who art in heaven . . ."

"Perdona nuestras ofensas…" – "Forgive us our trespasses"

"El nacimiento de Jesucristo fue de esta manera . . ." –

"Now the birth of Jesus was in this wise . . ." (Matthew 1)

"Apartaos de mí." – "Depart from me." (Matthew 7:23)

Señora – Missus

avion – airplane

Dia de los Muertos – Days of the Dead

Latin Words

"Dominus pascit me nihil mihi deerit: in loco pascuae facit: Me Ducit aquas quietis . . ."

(Psalm 23:1,2) "The Lord is my shepherd; He makes me to lie down in green pastures: He leads me beside the still waters."

PHOTOGRAPHS

Fernando (age 10) and Pablo (age 6)

Fernando (age 15)

First Church in Santa Martha (1993)

Fernando and Christy (2004)

First House

Picking up Children for VBS at Pokchik

VBS at Tayabts'en

Christy Teaching a Bible Lesson

Fernando's Aunt Walking to Bible Study

Working on the Bible Translation

ABOUT THE AUTHOR

As a child, Yvonne Blake heard stories of David Livingstone, Mary Slessor, and Hudson Taylor. Later, she taught many of those same missionary stories to other children, but her choice of new ones was very limited. She knew God was still doing marvelous and exciting works around the world, yet not many stories were being written or published.

At a translation workshop, Yvonne heard Fernando Angeles give his testimony of how God drew him and taught him about salvation by faith alone. Yvonne knew that God wanted her to write Fernando's story.

At times, she would get discouraged because of intermittent communication, but God would bring Fernando and Christy back into her path and encourage her to keep pressing forward to complete the book.

Yvonne prays that this story will be a tool to bring others to God. She hopes it will impress on young people the great need to translate the Bible into tribal languages, so that seeking souls may read and understand God's Word for themselves.

To order more books or donate to the Ténee Bible translation, email – polliwogpages@gmail.com or write to –

Polliwog Pages

4 Amy Lois Lane

Searsport, ME 04974

Made in the USA
Middletown, DE
17 June 2016